SOMETHING HAS HAPP

Something has happened to Joe. Now he doesn't feel safe; he feels sick, wants to cry and can't even concentrate on his computer games.

This carefully and sensitively written storybook has been created to enable conversations around safeguarding, teaching children about their right to feel safe, and what to do if, like Joe, they ever need help. With colourful and engaging illustrations, the story offers opportunities for discussion throughout, using Joe as a tool to help children understand their difficult feelings, who they can go to for help, and what they can do when it feels like nobody is listening.

This storybook:

- Teaches children about the right to feel safe, the safety continuum, networks of support and persistence

- Offers advice that can be used by children in any situation, from disclosing abuse to talking about smaller worries

- Can be used with both primary and lower-secondary aged pupils as a whole class, in small groups or in one-to-one sessions

Designed to be used alongside the professional guidebook, *A Practical Resource for Supporting Children's Right to Feel Safe*, this is an essential tool for teachers, support staff and other professionals who want to teach children that being safe from harm is the most important right they have, and that the trusted adults around them will always take action to believe and protect them.

Liz Bates is an independent education consultant. She supports both primary and secondary schools in all aspects of Emotional Health and Wellbeing, and Safeguarding, including whole school approaches, training staff and delivering talks to parents. Liz is a Protective Behaviours Trainer, a Wellbeing Award Advisor for Optimus and a regular contributor at national conferences.

Something Has Happened

Supporting Children's Right to Feel Safe

Liz Bates

Illustrated by Nigel Dodds

Routledge
Taylor & Francis Group

LONDON AND NEW YORK

First published 2022
by Routledge
2 Park Square, Milton Park, Abingdon, Oxon OX14 4RN

and by Routledge
605 Third Avenue, New York, NY 10158

Routledge is an imprint of the Taylor & Francis Group, an informa business

British Library Cataloguing-in-Publication Data
A catalogue record for this book is available from the British Library

Library of Congress Cataloging-in-Publication Data
Names: Bates, Liz, author. | Dodds, Nigel (Archaeological illustrator), illustrator.
Title: Something has happened : supporting children's right to feel safe /
Liz Bates : illustrated by Nigel Dodds.
Description: Abingdon, Oxon ; New York, NY : Routledge, 2022. |
Summary: Dealing with difficult emotions, Joe feels safe knowing
that he has persistence and a network of support.
Identifiers: LCCN 2021020279 (print) | LCCN 2021020280 (ebook) |
ISBN 9781032069203 (paperback) | ISBN 9781003204541 (ebook)
Subjects: CYAC: Safety—Fiction. | Emotional problems—Fiction.
Classification: LCC PZ7.1.B37725 So 2022 (print) | LCC PZ7.1.B37725 (ebook) |
DDC [Fic]—dc23
LC record available at https://lccn.loc.gov/2021020279
LC ebook record available at https://lccn.loc.gov/2021020280

ISBN: 978-1-032-06920-3 (pbk)
ISBN: 978-1-003-20454-1 (ebk)

DOI: 10.4324/9781003204541

Typeset in Apple Casual
by codeMantra

Joe doesn't feel safe.

Joe feels upset.

Something has happened.

What might that be?

1

Joe feels upset.

How does that feel?

How might Joe's body feel?

Joe feels shaky.

Joe feels sick.

Joe feels like crying.

Joe has butterflies in his tummy.

Joe can feel his heart beating fast.

Can you think of any other feelings
Joe might have in his body?

Joe can remember other times
when his body has felt like this.

On his first day
at a new school.

Gaming
with
his friends.

Riding his bike
downhill, really
fast.

Reading in
assembly.

4 But this is different.

Because....

Joe was **excited** to be going to a new school.

Joe plays on his console for **fun**.

Joe **chose** to ride his bike down the hill.

Joe was nervous but **wanted** to read in assembly.

Yes, this is different.

So Joe tries to forget about his feelings
by doing other things.

He plays with his friends.

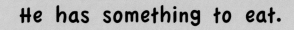

He has something to eat.

He plays more games.

He goes to visit
his nan.

What other things could Joe try?

But Joe's feelings don't go away.

They always come back when he thinks about what has happened.

He feels shaky when he plays with his friends.

He feels sick when he tries to eat.

He gets angry when he is on his console.

He feels like crying when he is at nan's house.

8

Joe wonders what to do.

What do you think he could do?

Can you help Joe?

Joe could talk to someone.

Someone he trusts.

Someone he feels safe with.

Someone who could help him.

It might be an adult at home.

It might be an adult at school.

It might be another adult he knows.

It might be a friend.

Who else might Joe talk to?

These are the people that Joe has chosen
to be on his network.

His network is made up of people Joe trusts.
People Joe feels safe with.

Dad, an
adult at
home.

Ms Lopez,
an adult
at school.

Aneeta, an
adult he
knows.

Mr Cooper,
another
adult he
knows.

Joe chose these people for other reasons too.

Dad is easy to contact because Joe

sees him every day.

So if Joe chose this person to speak to,

he could do it straight away.

Ms Lopez is a good listener and she always
believes the children in her class.
Once when Sara was being teased,
Ms Lopez took Sara's worries seriously.
So if Joe chose this person,
Joe knows he would be listened to.

Aneeta is Joe's friend's mum
and is really good at solving problems.
When Joe's friend Asha lost her dog,
Aneeta made posters and put them up
in the town.
So if Joe chose this person,
he knows that they would try to help.

Mr Cooper is Joe's next-door neighbour
and knows other ways to get help.
Once Joe's family were locked
out of their house.
Mr Cooper knew who to contact, and gave
everyone tea and cake while they
waited for help.
So if Joe chose this person, he knows
that they would get the right person to help.

Joe went to talk to
Dad but he
was going shopping.

Now what can Joe do?

Joe didn't give up.

He has more people on his network.

Joe went to talk to
Mr Cooper but he
wasn't in.

Joe didn't give up.

Joe went to talk to
Aneeta but she
was on the phone.

Joe didn't give up.

Joe went to talk to Ms Lopez
but she was talking to Mr Kumar.

Now what?

Joe wondered what to do.

Everyone seems so busy.

What could Joe do?

He could give up.

Or...

Joe speaks to his friends Josh and Sophie.
They know what to do.

Josh tells Joe that it is sometimes ok
to break the rules. In an emergency.

Sophie says this is an emergency
because Joe feels so bad.

Sophie tells Joe that it is ok
to interrupt adults in an emergency.

Josh tells Joe it is ok to keep asking
for help until someone listens.

Sophie and Josh say they will go
with Joe to interrupt Ms Lopez.

Ms Lopez didn't mind being interrupted.

She thanked Josh and Sophie for helping Joe.

Ms Lopez and Joe sat down.

Joe talked and Ms Lopez listened.

Joe told Ms Lopez how he was feeling.

Feeling sick, wanting to cry,

and all his other feelings.

23

Ms Lopez said Joe's feelings are very important.

She said it is ok to cry.

She said Joe had done the right thing by telling her how he feels.

Joe told Ms Lopez why he was upset,
and Ms Lopez said she would try
to help him.

Joe was glad he talked with Ms Lopez.

He stopped feeling so shaky.

He didn't feel quite so sick anymore.

He didn't feel like crying.

Most of the butterflies had flown away.

His heart stopped beating quite so fast.

Joe felt happier and calmer because

he had talked with an adult he trusts.

Joe knew that Ms Lopez would do all

that she could to help him.

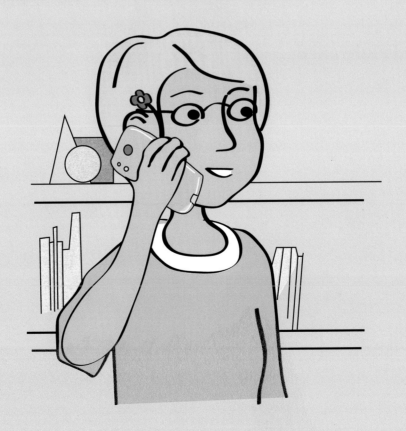

Nothing can change the things that upset Joe.

Not every day can be a good day.

But now Joe knows what he can do

if he feels upset...

or worried...

or frightened...

or alone...

or sad.

Joe wanted to tell his story just in case
you ever need help like he did.

Just in case something has happened to you.

Because there will be someone you can talk
with, and you can talk with that someone
about anything, even if it is a big thing
or a small thing.

29

And now you know what to do.